The Teaching of the Spirit.

A BRIEF MEMOIR

OF

GEORGE TYRRELL, B.A.,

LATE OF TRIN. COLL., CANT.

BY

CLAUDE S. BIRD, B.A.

"Is not my word like as a fire? saith the Lord; and like a hammer that breaketh the rock in pieces?"—Jer. xxiii. 29.

LONDON:
JAMES NISBET AND CO., 21 BERNERS STREET.
M.DCCC.LXI.

EDINBURGH:
PRINTED BY BALLANTYNE AND COMPANY,
PAUL'S WORK.

PREFACE.

THIS narrative was compiled with a view to private circulation, and is now published by request of the friends of the humble Christian who forms its subject. His life was quiet, and devoid of striking incidents, excepting that of his conversion from infidelity to the faith of Christ; yet afforded an unusually bright example of the sanctifying power of the Holy Spirit, which adorned with the graces of holiness a character of uncommon natural beauty. No less did it illustrate the quickness and power of the Sword of the Spirit. God vindicated the divine Word against his unbelief, by it converted the soul, made it the sole lamp to his feet, and led him by its light from strength to strength, till he appeared before God in Zion.

An unfinished autobiography and large correspondence have furnished the chief materials, personal recollections of the writer and other college friends the rest. It has been a sweet though sad pleasure to frame this imperfect record, which is now commended to the kind attention of readers, and the blessing of God. May it kindle new thoughts and aspirations in many breasts; may it encourage believers steadfastly to follow him, who through faith and patience inherits the promises; finally, may it serve to exalt that abundant grace of Christ which the subject of this memoir so richly experienced, and which he strove while living to proclaim to all men!

CONTENTS.

I.

Early Life.

EARLY LIFE.

GEORGE TYRRELL was a younger son of a gentleman of honourable position and easy circumstances. He was born January 26, 1835. The following is his own account of his childhood:—"I had some religious impressions—I can call them no more—stamped on my mind in early childhood by my mother, who died before I was nine years old; but these were of a very imperfect kind; they amounted to an acknowledgment of a God, a degree of reverence for the Bible, but an Unitarian view of the Divinity of our Lord Jesus Christ. Insomuch that I remember at a very early age arguing with some poor servants in our family against the Divinity of Jesus Christ, shewing them the text, 'My Father is greater than I,' (John xiv.,) which I thought very conclusive, and was not a little vain of displaying my powers in adducing.

"Between the ages of ten and fifteen, I was at a private school. Here during my whole stay I was without God in the world. I learnt the collect and epistle and went to church, and read first in my Latin and afterwards my Greek Testament, learning passages by heart, (which, by the way, as if sticking in the throat of such a sinner, always gave me a difficulty which I could not at all account for, and often lost me places in my class which I was very loth to sacrifice,) but I had no kind of really Christian instruction, as far as I can judge in the retrospect; and became, as my mind opened out, from being a godless child, a sceptical and unbelieving boy.

"During this time my corrupt and wicked heart had sunk me into the lowest degradation. I did, I believe, mumble over some words of prayer night and morning, but never read the Bible by myself—I did not, in fact, believe it. Indeed, shocking to relate, I induced my most intimate friend, who up to this time had retained some religious impressions, to follow my example, and become, as alas! he has remained, an infidel. I well remember that when it became incumbent on me to be confirmed, my conscience smote me; but I persuaded myself that I had no course but to go through it as a form, being, as I believe, afraid to announce publicly to my master that I was an infidel.

"There are two circumstances that I must not neglect to mention, in addition to what I have related of this period of my life. I was an enthusiastic admirer of nature and poetic visionary. I used to compose poems in great numbers; and it was the aspiration of my ambitious heart rather to be great as a poet, than in any active path of worldly aggrandizement. I was industrious all this time, and was, for the year and a half before I left the school, at the head of it; and it gave great scope, as I but too well remember, to an ambitious and emulous desire to outstrip even the humble competitors of a private school, numbering hardly forty boys.

"But the other circumstance which I wished particularly to mention, was my exceeding wretchedness at school. Looking back on my childhood and boyhood, I find that the earliest characteristic, next to that of its innate wickedness, was its almost uniform unhappiness. Well do I recollect lying in my little cot, when almost a baby, a prey to the most horribly ghastly and superstitious imaginations; and on another occasion awaking at night in such great distress as to cause me to exclaim, with the sonorous but most heartfelt cry of 'Oh, Jane, Jane!' (the name of my nurse) 'no tongue can tell what I endure.' This, as may be well supposed, formed for long after a favourite topic for banter among my family. I could mention many other little things of the same kind, (such as a resolve never to smile again,) which, however apparently trifling, were associated with feelings of most bitter grief. I have thought that had such wickedness as mine been accompanied by anything less of suffering, I could never have been reclaimed."

Here follows a description of the cruelty of his school-fellows, and his consequent sufferings, especially through a betrayal of confidence which deeply wounded his tender, sensitive feelings. Then an account of one boy in particular, whom he dreaded above all.

"The misery his cruelty sometimes occasioned me cannot be expressed by too strong a term; it was torture, it was anguish of soul, it was agony. And oh! as I recall these things my heart is lifted up with adoration. There when I, poor helpless child, was sitting in the bitterness of my soul, crying out, but finding no comforter, there stood Jesus looking on me with unutterable love, with His heart yearning over me, saying, 'I have loved thee with an everlasting love, therefore with loving-kindness am I drawing thee.' Wonderful Saviour! preparing me in some inscrutable and mysterious way, by these early lessons, for that manifestation of unfathomable love which He was to make to my soul in due time."

II.

Infidelity.

INFIDELITY.

In 1850, and at the age of fifteen, Tyrrell proceeded to Rugby School, where he remained four years. He became happier there, and less openly wicked, "but the unclean spirit only kept itself quiet for awhile, whilst it served its master's purpose." He continues—"I now began to be actuated by a spirit of worldly aggrandizement and emulation, together with desire of literary distinction and emulation, which it is indeed by a masterpiece of his craft that Satan has persuaded his votaries to look upon as not only innocent but praiseworthy."

The writer first saw Tyrrell at Rugby in 1851, and was prepossessed by his quiet, gentlemanly appearance. He was then just reaching the Sixth Form, in which he distinguished himself by his classical knowledge, elegance of mind, and steady diligence. He gained many prizes, and finally one of the chief honours, called Exhibitions. I never heard him found fault with, nor was he often corrected in any mistake; but his regularity and accuracy confirmed the judgment of a phrenologist, who pronounced his bump of order very large. He was well read in history and general literature. He shewed a cultivated taste in art, in an excursion made with myself and another to the manufactories of Birmingham, which we all enjoyed. He was generally respected, and much liked by some. His attendance at public worship was regular; and I have even seen him at the Lord's Table, in manner reverent; but it may have been once only. It was difficult to know by his outward life whether he were led of the Spirit or not. His manners were always gentle and refined, his feelings warm and affectionate. A highly sensitive temperament added to what I may term the delicacy of his character. A quick temper and occasional sarcasms were almost his only visible faults. His sincerity was remarkable; he would have scorned to lie. But how little did all this avail in the sight of God! and even in his own sight at a later period! How vain are human morals, without the first and great commandment influencing the heart!

God was gradually leading him, however, to the

knowledge of the truth, as he used afterwards to acknowledge; comparing this part of his life with the wanderings of Israel in the wilderness, and dwelling with peculiar affection on Deuteronomy xxxii., where God's tender care of His helpless yet cherished people is so beautifully illustrated. The writings of S. T. Coleridge, though they have proved pernicious to other minds, did much to solve his doubts of the truth of Christianity. He admired the New Testament, though the Old remained to him a complete puzzle.

An animated discussion took place one evening between himself and a clever school-fellow, in which Tyrrell maintained that the raising up of the Duke of Wellington for the overthrow of Napoleon, was an *extraordinary* exertion of Almighty Power in behalf of national justice. This distinct recognition of the free and special providence of God, shews that he was under very serious impressions. For the civilized world in general has no such clear view of Providence, especially in boyhood. The fool saith in his heart, "There is no God." The disputants settled that their difference was verbal only, since nothing could be *hard* to God; but that the coincidence of the crisis which demanded, and the providence which furnished, a Wellington, was certainly unusual, and in that sense extraordinary. It is not often that schoolboy disputes end with so much good sense and credit to both parties. But to unfold the dark picture drawn by his own hand:—

"I was now, as I thought, satisfied of the falsehood, that is, the human origin, of the Christian religion. But I was by no means satisfied as to what was to be substituted in its place. In fact, I was in all my leisure hours continually guessing at the riddle of truth. Many were the books that I journeyed through, comprising many of the alas! too numerous and too pernicious infidel publications of the time. It has often put me in mind of that line in Virgil describing Dido's lonely and cheerless rambles in the shades below—'Longam incomitata videtur Ire viam.' Long and lonely, indeed, were the wanderings that my poor blind soul passed through, in the comfortless regions of intellectual speculation; but ah! with a gentle, and patient, and tender Saviour all the while watching my steps, leading me on, from blindness to blindness, by a way that I knew not, and giving me just such faint strugglings of light as were to serve to bring me to the time when He was to be revealed to my soul, and the light of heaven burst full on my view.

"But, meanwhile, though I was being followed and tended by this unknown Shepherd, there was another master, whose I was, and whom I served. This cruel and wicked master I served none the less effectually, because I imagined that his very existence was a fable. I absolutely had no more belief in the existence of Satan at this time, than in the existence of Jupiter, or any other of the heathen gods; and, consequently, I was his most active and devoted servant. I fear that long after I myself was plucked as a brand from the burning, the arguments I employed, with one at least of my companions, may have had their fatal effects continued. It is true that I did not make a matter of public boast of my infidelity, but was rather willing that it should escape notice, though not shrinking from the avowal in case of the question being put to me, as I think it hardly ever was put, point blank. In point of fact, I daily acted the hypocrite, though this was softened over to my conscience, as being a matter of school discipline which I must perform. I refer, for instance, to joining in the services at church, and in prayers in the private boarding-house. The Holy Communion, indeed, I was mercifully preserved, I believe almost without exception, during my course at Rugby, from desecrating. And I remember it was a severe trial to my feelings, having to walk out as a kind of culprit amongst the careless and profane of the boys, who from less definite motives shunned the table of the Lord.

"Nor was I, during the latter part of my stay at Rugby, without some slight stirrings, as I believe, of the Holy Spirit within me: or, perhaps I should say, that my enthralled soul was making some pitiable groans after the freedom of the sons of God, which it was so utterly powerless to attain. Some year and a half before I left Rugby, I was laid up during a winter vacation with a lame knee, injured in a game at football, which confined me for a long time chiefly to the house. This additional occasion for being engrossed in self, as the affliction proved, when I was not yet under the teaching of the Spirit, so wrapped me up in my own pursuits, as to elicit a very well-merited reproof for selfishness from my sister. This had so much effect on me as to wring me with very acute sensations of self-recrimination and mortified self-love, to throw me into bitter tears, and to occasion some transient endeavours after amendment, accompanied, I believe, with a degree of dumb, dark prayer.

"An incident occurred at Rugby some considerable time before this, which will illustrate my sad spiritual condition whilst there. I had on principle at that time given up private prayer, under the deluded conviction that it was absurd to suppose that such a being as God could be induced to alter His proceedings for the prayers of such a creature as myself—the miserable sophistry into which I had been beguiled. One night, accordingly, in my bedroom, one of my school-fellows, who bore me no good feeling, stuck up a piece of paper on the wall,—there were four or five other boys in the same bedroom,—containing a written request that I would say my prayers. The boy who wrote this was one who, if he said prayers himself, was not actuated in his request by any other motive than that of mortifying me. And so much did it sting me to the quick, and shame me, that I followed the injunction, and thenceforth never omitted kneeling down with my face buried in my hands. Sometimes I did repeat words of prayer, at other times a flood of worldly thoughts were all my meditation. I trust the humiliation was a salutary one.

"One other incident I will mention. Dr Goulburn, in one of his sermons, said that it would be an ample reward to him for his pains in preaching, if only one of his hearers should remember his words at some future day of trial and turn to God, or something of that kind. This had so much effect on me, that it induced me to offer up a sincere prayer that God would be pleased to bring me through some grievous affliction, if such were necessary for my eternal well-being. Thus did He make me send up this dumb cry, that when His answer came to pass I might believe.

"As to the nature of my infidelity, it was singularly complete in its darkness. I considered the Bible to be an uninspired composition of certain human authors. Jesus Christ I considered a simply good and great man, not without a secret and ill-defined contempt for the mildness and gentleness of His holy character." . . . . "I held the miracles to be the imaginations and exaggerations of a succeeding age.

I held the coming judgment of mankind before Christ's tribunal a most unfounded creation of man's fancy. The strongest language I can use cannot overstate the complete scorn and ridicule with which I regarded the very supposition of the existence of Satan. I was a most willing scoffer at the doctrine of original sin. In my arrogance, I really supposed that hardly any persons but myself were in the habit of reflecting on all these things, and that those few who did were of the same opinion with myself in secret. I was effectually blinded as to the existence of hell and of eternal punishment. I should at any time have died without any other feeling than that of being loth to leave this world, and uncertain as to what was to follow. It was regarded by my mind as simply taking a plunge out of a lighted room into the obscure night without. I liked the comfortable light, and was averse to being thus turned out into the dark. But that comprises all the objection that I felt to the thought of death. I could go into a thunderstorm, a dark walk by night, a rough sea in a boat, and all without any more apprehension as to what might follow death, than has the beast that perisheth.

"This will but too amply prove that I was hitherto in darkness, yea, the very blackness of darkness, the comfortless land of the valley of the shadow of death; making indeed some poor efforts to feel after God, but without hope, without God in the world; an alien from the commonwealth of Israel; an outcast on the face of society, neither consorting with the openly and avowedly bad, nor received,—of course far, far from it,—by the excellent of the earth; a monstrosity, an astonishment; in the bondage of Satan and of sin; a blasphemer and a crucifier of Christ; I was made to 'dwell in darkness, as those that have been long dead.'"

III.

Conversion.

CONVERSION.

With these words concludes the unfinished narrative, commenced with the purpose of "recording, in reliance on the aid of the Holy Spirit, and to the glory of God's infinite mercy in Christ Jesus to the chief of sinners, some of the circumstances of his conversion from infidelity to the gospel of Jesus Christ during the autumn of 1854." It appears, therefore, to be rather in conformity with his own wishes, than a violation of privacy, to have transcribed most of it here. Happily a written continuation of it is at hand, in a letter addressed to a poor young man, dying unconverted, of whom some further account will be given below.

The scene is laid in Tyrrell's own home, where, apart from all religious friends and ministers, "the Lord alone did lead him." He had left Rugby school, to prepare for his intended course at the University of Cambridge. Perhaps his heart had been softened by the loss of a near relative whom he loved and esteemed very highly. I say the heart, for infidelity in this age and country is a thing of the heart; its essence is pride and obstinacy, not mental weakness or ignorance.

"It pleased God to incline me by His Holy Spirit to pray earnestly to Him, and to study the Bible. The more I read the Bible, and the more I prayed, the more a new and heavenly light began to fall upon the pages of Holy Scripture. After a while I began to see, as clearly as the daylight, that this book, which I had so long been unable to understand, was indeed the Word of the living God. I saw that Jesus Christ had been sent by God to die for the sins of the world. I was moved by the Spirit of God to wash away my sins in Christ's blood by faith; and then I felt like a little child who has returned to his father's arms. I wept over the sins of my past life, and I began to feel what it was to have peace with God. I felt that God was now no longer *an unknown God*, and I knew that He was now *my God*, and this gave me unutterable joy.

"For about a fortnight after this, I had the most heavenly joy and peace, in having at last found out the true God, and in finding that the great riddle, as it were, which had been so long puzzling me, was made clear. My emotion, however, at this joyful discovery was so great, that it became after a while too much for me, and I was attacked with a violent brain fever. For many days I lay at death's door, in a continual delirium; but after I had gone through much agonizing suffering, it pleased God to raise me up again. Ever since then I have been on the whole improving in health, but have never to this day recovered the shock upon my constitution. But though the time of which I write is now between four and five years ago, I have even to this day and at this moment the same peace and joy that I got then for the first time, only more sobered down; and I still find the same light shining on the Bible, only a more quiet, steady light. Since then I have been taught many things in the midst of grievous trials. The great things that I have learned are these: that I am, in myself, utterly ruined by sin; that God is the same faithful Father that I first found Him to be; and that Jesus Christ is the same faithful and mighty Saviour.

"Now, dear friend, when I write you these things,

I write you the plain truth, a plain simple account of things that really happened. I am told that you are not unacquainted with this Bible of which I speak. I invite you to pray for this same Holy Spirit, and you shall find its pages as full of light as I did and do: I invite you to wash in the same blood of Jesus Christ which cleanseth from all sin, and you shall find your sins washed away as mine have been: I invite you to return to the arms of the same tender heavenly Father as I returned to, and you shall find Him to be no less loving."

What an instance of the quickness and power of the sword of the Spirit is exhibited in this narrative! Like that of every true conversion, it discredits two common and opposite errors. Many trust to Christ for safety in willing ignorance of the Scriptures, and with a blind affection, as they would have trusted to the human mediators of the Church of Rome, if directed to them. Like the misguided worshippers of the Virgin Mary, they rejoice in "getting peace," and mistake their relieved, confiding feelings for the witness of the Spirit. Their faith, if faith at all, is most dishonouring to God. Others mistake an understanding, newly enlightened with regard to the gospel of Christ, for an acceptance of Him, and a saving change of heart. But Tyrrell had been led to diligent study of the written truth, with prayer; and the same Spirit who moved him to this recommended the truth of Christ both to his understanding and to his heart. He then intelligently accepted Christ as his own, cast all his sins on Him, and loved Him thenceforth with all his *heart* and all his *mind*.

It is also to be remarked, in this conversion, that God dispensed entirely with human teachers. Tyrrell believed that this was designed to make him place his whole reliance upon God and His Word in future life. It led him to prize the Scriptures far more than is common among God's children, just as Luther did, after his similar experience of their power. He saw an evidence of their divine origin in the fact that the Holy Spirit had, as it were, held the key of them, shutting them against the proud heart, unfolding their depths to humble prayer.

So complete was the triumph over his former contemptuous infidelity respecting the Old Testament, that he paid it far more honour than most believing readers do, reading it through and through with minute care. He had once despised the Old Testament as inferior to the New, and entirely disconnected from it. Now he would speak often with wonder and delight of the marvellous unity in diversity of the whole sacred volume, which has met every varying want and suited every circumstance of believers in all ages, and yet bears throughout the impress of one concerting Agent, in whose combined melodies Christ Jesus our Redeemer returns again and again, through successive strains and movements, as the sweet and all-pervading theme.

Whenever he found a passage that appealed strongly to his feelings, or cast a new light on any subject, he always repeated it to his friends as if it were a new treasure, talking of it, writing of it, till he had indelibly fixed its words upon his memory, and its lessons on his heart. And he ever read Scripture in order to feed the heart, not to fill the head; he sought to realize all spiritually, and to *live* thereby.

He used to refuse all commentaries, except for rare occasional reference; and if the want of health did not permit him to read much at any period, he would lay aside all volumes but that one most dear and pure, the field wherein he had discovered with such joy the pearl of great price, and whose cultivation daily repaid him with new treasures, gems of that wisdom which is more precious than rubies.

But he could not keep these riches locked within his breast. In season and out of season he laboured to bring others to Christ. In his walks he used to seize any opportunity of interrupting his communion with Jesus, whose companionship he vividly realized when alone, to speak of salvation through Him to any passing stranger. These wayside conversations were frequently blessed in later days. An infidel at Cambridge was silenced,—a young and inquiring Jew at Exeter was much struck,—by what was thus said.

Taking shelter one day in a shed near London, Tyrrell found a painter engaged in removing paint from wood by means of bulls' blood. He made it a parable to point to the removal of sin by the blood of Christ. "But there is another way of taking it off, sir," said the painter; "we sometimes *burn it off*." And then Tyrrell reminded him of the one awful alternative—Christ's blood, or the fire that is never quenched. He was heard with attention, and the parable could not easily be forgotten.

Sometimes his abrupt address to a stranger, as, "Sir, are you prepared to meet your God?" might offend, but even then it could not fail to impress. In general, his gentle, humble love and kindness disarmed all hostility. But he considered offence unavoidable in the execution of his duty to the unconverted, by speaking boldly of sin and a Saviour. He took it on himself as the necessary offence of the cross, as part of the reproach of Christ, never to cease, which he truly counted an honour.

On the other hand, he shunned the society of the worldly after his conversion, fearing that, instead of benefiting them, he should injure himself. In so acting he was guided by Scripture, and if he erred in excessive retirement, and silence in the presence of the thoughtless, he erred on the right side. He felt weak, easily tempted into unspirituality and worldliness, though this could not be known by others. And having been so recently pulled out of the fire, he wisely feared to venture near it again. "Young Christians," he writes, "have much of the *Parthian* mode of fighting."

IV.

College Life.

COLLEGE LIFE.

This rule of conduct led Tyrrell into a very quiet, secluded life at Trinity College, Cambridge, whither he now removed on the restoration of his health. But the good hand of his God was with him, providing him with friends of singularly pure and earnest piety in his own college and academic year. He welcomed these brethren in Christ with deep and new-felt joy. His strong affection flowed forth towards them all with Christ-like tenderness. Seven of them, including himself, formed a Bible party for Saturday-evening meetings, which afforded much sweet communion on heavenly things to the united members of this little family. Three have now rejoined their Head in Paradise; four are yet militant on earth; but the little family is still one—"we are seven." All doubtless remember with hallowed pleasure their once-valued meetings, anticipating the reunion of all in perfect love and unfettered communion.

Tyrrell's health remained very uncertain ever after his illness; bodily weakness and fluctuating nerves exposed him to much trial. Gratefully did he take this bitter cup, although longing to regain health, if God should see fit; which he speaks of in a letter as, according to an old saying, "the greatest of earthly blessings,—*except sickness.*" He had narrowly escaped from a mind permanently diseased by his brain fever; and his weak head gave him much trouble, while it permitted but little study. It very nearly gave way altogether during his second year at college; the result being a second severe illness, and extreme distress of mind for months afterwards. According to his own account, he had declined in piety before this illness came to correct him. He sank into the depths beneath its pressure, unable to recover his priceless but lost view of the reconciled face of God. But the lesson was effectually taught, how evil a thing it is and bitter to forsake the Lord our God. The experience now required to enforce it was never afterwards repeated. Two years later he thus describes this illness:—"*Then* I passed through tribulation without the presence and peace of the Lord Jesus, *now with*—and oh, the difference!

πολὺ τὸ μέσον. *Then* the torrent of ungodliness and corruption swept unimpeded over my soul; I was helpless, utterly helpless. *Now* the same flood has been swelling up, but the Spirit of the Lord has lifted up a standard against it. The Lord Jesus has not disappointed me, in giving me His uninterrupted peace deep down in my soul, beyond the reach of the darts of Satan and the corruption of my own most wicked heart. *Then* I could not read the Bible, nor pray, except on going into bed every night, out of the despair and bitterness of my soul, 'God be merciful to me.' I never got beyond that. *Now* the Lord has enabled me, by His grace, to pray more earnestly and more constantly than at any other period of my life, and to retain my hold on and enjoyment of His Word."

Is not the change here described encouraging to the tempted Christian? The second of these trials was very severe. "I have been still passing," he writes, "through a time of sharp conflict and temptation. The last two months seem to me, in point of duration, much more like two years." Yet hear how he continues: "But I have felt that the Lord has been doing His work in my soul. He has been exceeding good to me, more so than I can ever describe, bearing with me, forgiving me, comforting me, shewing me His presence, and strengthening me."

What a contrast to the former scene! The text he loved was already fulfilled in him—"When He hath tried me, I shall come forth as gold." Dross never again separated him from the presence of Christ, although its remains demanded long-continued refining, repeated heatings in the furnace of affliction, before he became a vessel unto honour, pure, and meet for the Master's use in the courts of heaven.

Tyrrell called upon me soon after my arrival in Cambridge, October 1856, two years later than himself. The Memoir of the Mackenzies lay on my table, and I ventured to remark on the lovely character of Frank Mackenzie, that, though almost inborn with him, it might be attained by others in the strength of the Holy Spirit. This immediately tore away the veil from between us. I was astonished to see my friend's face flush with joy, his eyes sparkle, his quiet manner change into vivacity. He proceeded to tell me, in perfect confidence of sympathy, of the great change through which he had passed since we last met. I had heard of his conversion, but, in the heartless language of professors, as *religious excitement*,—a term still employed to cast discredit on every great and open work of God among human hearts. Laodicea will slander, if she cannot deny, the zeal that shames her.

But Tyrrell told me all the truth that afternoon; and I can never forget how our hearts burned within us as we talked together by the way. Jesus Himself was indeed, to use Tyrrell's own expression, "the blessed third." I mistook three miles of the Madingley Road for one, absorbed in the interest of his story, and delighted to have found so precious a friend at the outset of my college course. For he was a friend beyond price, living so near to the throne of God, and drawing all his companions thither, while ceaseless in prayer for them. Some of them were in danger of too abstract a religion, but his was exceedingly personal,—its substance being union with Christ by the Spirit, and access thereby to the Father. He was very faithful to his brothers in Christ, for his love to them was only second to his love to God. He valued very highly that union of God's children which Christ Himself prayed for in His last hours, and most earnestly interceded for it. He anticipated that the general outpouring of the Spirit would soon be followed by increased unity of heart and action, and that this union would be cemented by the attendant persecution which revived piety in the Church of Christ must attract. He hoped that in heaven we should find a "separate nook in our hearts" for every brother and sister there,—so wide was his fervent love. Those who knew him will be ready to adopt the language which he used respecting a departed friend about this time: —"It was such a gracious dealing of God's to me, to give me so sweet a friend, who was so soon to be taken to Himself."

The degree in which he realized communion with Jesus, and not less the fellowship of saints on earth, will be seen from the following letter, full of the tenderest sympathy, to a Christian friend, who had returned into the arms of Christ after wandering awhile, and found his lost communion restored:—

"MY VERY DEAR BROTHER,—'Rejoice in the Lord alway, and again I say, Rejoice.' Forgive me if I seem rather a fool on this occasion; 'if I be beside myself, it is to God.' I do indeed rejoice with you, my dear brother. Your letter was a source in me of the highest good that any human thing can produce—it made me glorify God on your behalf. This is one of the sweetest turns that the Lord Jesus has ever done me, to send me such really glad tidings from a dear brother. There was a certain sentence in your letter worth a thousand,—a sentence that sends thrills of joy through the angels of heaven. I mean this—'I had such sweet communion with Him as I never had before.' Sweet, my dear friend, are returning showers to the thirsty land, sweet is home to the weary traveller, sweet is cooling water to the hot tongue, but oh! sweeter far, in truth, is the flowing in again of the love of Jesus, on the soul that has been tossed and tried, and weary and dissatisfied, between the harassing of the world, the buffetings of Satan, the loneliness and emptiness of being left to itself without the society of the 'Beloved.'

"My dear brother, is it not sweet company to have Jesus near? to be able to call upon Him by His name, 'Jesus, my sweet Saviour, my God?' and to feel that He hears as if He were in the room? 'My Beloved is mine, and I am His.'"

The writer recalls to mind numberless little ways and sayings of his dear friend, which he must forbear to obtrude upon the reader. Many and many a scene and conversation is engraved upon his memory. Not least the college evening chapel-service, at which dear Tyrrell used to sit before the commencement with hands clasped upon his knees, his eyes not wandering around, but closed in prayer, and upturned within the trembling eye-lids, while his spirit was redeeming the time of delay, for the worship of his Father.

Perhaps his most favourite books were Rutherford's Letters, Hewitson's Remains, Newton's Life, and Cecil's Remains.

Amiable as he had been at school, there was now such a contrast to his former self,—not in his new tastes and spirituality alone, but also in moral character. His petulance had been exchanged for exceeding meekness and forbearance; his pride for self-renunciation before others, as well as before the Searcher of hearts; his satire had been subdued into quiet, stingless humour, which enlivened his serious but never gloomy talk. We need not fear to say that faults remained even in the outward man,—transient impatience, hastiness of judgment, too much confidence in a narrow experience, and too *little* in man, if this be possible. Yet these were very rarely visible, least of all in trying times, because then he prayed against them most, and overcame them in Christ's strength.

Inward sins his letters abundantly confess. He knew well the plague of his own heart, nor must it be denied here. But he kept up, through the Holy Spirit, a most unflinching conflict with it, crucifying it daily, nailing the body of sin to the cross of Christ by faith.

His watchfulness against Satan contrasted strongly with his former unbelief in the tempter; his realization of *answers* to prayer, as well as of the efficacy of prayer, with his once prayerless infidelity. He even kept lists of answers to prayer, that he might not omit to thank God for any of His gifts and blessings; nor deprive the Benefactor of the glory due for any of His benefits.

He expressed his belief at this period that he had lost in some degree the warmth of his first love to

Christ, and might recover it by prayer. He did so recover and increase it, that thenceforth every one might see that Jesus was his dearest friend. Might we not all do this if we would; instead of mourning vainly, perhaps idly, over the coldness of our hearts? God helps those that help themselves. But Tyrrell was never idle. He rose early in cold weather as regularly as in warm, to pray and read the Scriptures—which he often turned into prayer as he went along—for a long while before breakfast, that God might have all his first and best thoughts, and that heavenly things might gain early and lasting possession of his mind. Herein lay a chief secret of his holy walk.

Christ's person, character, and kingdom occupied his reflections frequently. He considered Christ's actual presence essential to the full happiness of His people, and for this and other reasons often prayed, "Thy kingdom come." "If ever," he writes, "you feel the trials of your situation heavier than usual upon you, I wish you would join with me in praying, Come, Lord Jesus." * The Jews also assumed

* He said to the writer one evening, after hearing Handel's Hallelujah Chorus sung in Trinity Chapel, and with reference to the triumphant song of Christ's kingdom there represented:

great importance in his future views and prayers. Often has he reminded his friends to pray for the peace of Jerusalem, and the Jews were rarely if ever passed over by him, in arranging for united prayer, or in his own supplications. He anticipated their restoration as very near at hand, and estimated it in the balance of Scripture as actually the cause of "life from the dead" to the world.

The mention of united prayer awakes many sacred recollections. Tyrrell instituted daily prayer with the writer while lodging in the same house in Cambridge, and also a weekly prayer-meeting with two or three friends on Friday evenings, for missions, the Jews, and the Church of Christ. But what especially characterized him was the usual request on many a passing occasion, "Will you offer a few words of prayer before we go?" A social evening, a happy hour of conversation, a little plan proposed, a visit to the tract-district, a religious meeting, and a hundred other such times, almost always elicited this request from him, and so were "sanctified by prayer." How much that single habit implied!

"I felt as if I could have thrown myself down, and rolled on the ground":—overwhelmed by the anticipation.

What blessings it brought down! What hallowed influence it gave to intercourse!

Before conversion, Tyrrell had been an intense admirer of Alfred Tennyson, and had aspired to becoming a poet himself. Afterwards he threw Tennyson's works and his own poetical aims aside on principle; and though good poetry kindled his warm admiration, hymns were far dearer to him. He was asked at college to write some lines in an album. Others had written in it favourite poetical pieces, but Tyrrell's choice took another direction; he preferred to honour Christ and express his own feelings in the well-known hymn:—

"When I survey the wondrous cross,
On which the Prince of glory died,
My richest gain I count but loss,
And pour contempt on all my pride."

No longer contemplating social and literary distinction, but the service of Christ, and the work of winning souls to Him as a preacher of the cross, he devoted his whole mind to understanding, glorifying, and testifying of Christ, of which the above incident is a characteristic instance.

He could testify, too, in the face of opposition or ridicule, though his sensitiveness caused him much pain in so doing. Meek in himself, he became bold when the honour of Christ demanded it. Coming late to dinner in Trinity Hall one Sunday afternoon, he could not find room near his own Christian friends as usual, but had to sit down among "fast" men. One of these used most offensive language, and repeated it till Tyrrell could bear it no longer, but turned to the man and addressed him in his most earnest manner, "I pray God, my friend, that your curses may never fall upon your own head." The man was struck dumb, and made no reply.

Letters of April 1857, indicate growth in grace and in the knowledge of our Lord and Saviour Jesus Christ.

"Jesus has been dealing with me this vacation in a way that I cannot declare: leading me onward into the knowledge of the intensity of His love. His ways are not our ways, nor His thoughts our thoughts. He hides His face from us for a small moment, and then crushes us with the weight of His blessed love. Truly His name is 'Wonderful.'"

Again:—"I have had sweeter draughts of Jesus' love this vacation, than ever since my first week of believing. He has come into my soul like the former and the latter rain. This I take as an earnest of yet richer showers. He has been talking to me of the '*peace*' which He promised to '*leave with*' His disciples—of the joy that no man taketh from you."

Early in 1857, Tyrrell took a tract-district in the village of Chesterton, near Cambridge. To this charge he warmly devoted himself, so far as time and the need of exercise allowed. He kept up special preparation and united prayer before visiting, and latterly visited twice and even thrice in the week, to gain more time for individual conversation with all his cottagers. He also shared a cottage-lecture in Chesterton with the writer.

In one case, he was manifestly blessed, being permitted to lead a soul to Christ. A poor butcher was dying of consumption, at the age of forty, whose heart, so long estranged from God, could not easily be reconciled to Him on the death-bed. He was truly penitent; but endured what he called the terrors of the Lord. Probably this anguish, and temptation of Satan, was permitted, to deter others from death-bed repentance. Weeks followed weeks, during which all instruction and comfort appeared to be lost on the sufferer; his soul could find no rest. But Tyrrell continued to visit him very frequently, and to wait upon God, till, at last, the penitent realized his acceptance with Christ, and enjoyed that peace of God, which passeth all understanding. Then Tyrrell was glad indeed; and called on all his friends to rejoice with him.

In a few days more the poor man died in the faith of Christ; so that the work was complete, and Tyrrell's visits were no longer needed, in the good providence of God, just when they must have ceased, through his leaving Cambridge. This was the plainest instance of successful ministry. But other hearts in that district were deeply touched, and one of the worst quite softened, by the words of love and faithfulness. May they never be forgotten!

Leaving Cambridge, in June 1857, for the long vacation, Tyrrell spent a few weeks at home, and then proceeded with a relative to Bangor, for the sake of the air. Here he lodged a long time; and, being ever busy for the Master, formed friendships with pious persons in different ranks of life. Especially cherished was his friendship with one poor old woman, whose thoughts and language appear to have been singularly refined by her piety, and afforded him continual pleasure. He often repeated afterwards one of her remarks, that God was so kind to her in every little thing, that it seemed as if He had no one else in the world to care for.

She was a child of God indeed, and rich in faith; full of praise, and one of "the Lord's remembrancers." With her he used to correspond till her death. She knitted him a pair of red mittens before Christmas, and sent them to him at Cambridge, in proof of her gratitude. He came into the writer's rooms with them in his hands, and such pleasure beaming in his face, to tell of the present. Much merriment did those red mittens create, and made him happier than if the Queen had sent them. So truly did he "condescend to men of low estate," and so little did the distinctions of this life appear to him, when he found grace present in the heart. He realized the communion of saints, and the sweetness of that tie by which faith in one Saviour unites *all* the children of God.

He could bear with peculiar and defective Christians, and love them in the truth. "They are like little bits of broken looking-glass," he used to say, "which are all of different shapes and sizes, yet all reflect and sparkle in the sun. And so all Christians reflect Christ, though in various ways, and though unlike each other. Each is a member of Christ, though some are little members; and even the little members have each their own peculiar work and office, which no other member could perform."

He had conversed and prayed much with one brother in Christ, most amiable, yet weak in faith, whom it pleased God to take to Himself. He thus expresses his affection and kind judgment on hearing of the event:—

"It filled me with that sweet feeling of sorrowful joy and thanksgiving with which we may well hear of our brethren being laid aside to sleep a little while, till they come with Christ in glory. Looking back on my intercourse with dear V—— H——, I cannot help recognizing that his was the spirit of one that pleased God; and so God took him. I remember his gentle cheerfulness and sweetness, want of self-consciousness, humility, and heavenly-mindedness; and think that it is good for him to be with Jesus. These things I saw not so clearly while he was still with us; for I wanted a greater degree of likeness to him to appreciate him better. But now that the Lord has set His seal to it, I admire His ways, and see that our brother was fit to be laid asleep. It humbled me before Him with an indescribable feeling of joy and gratitude to think that He had allowed me to see so much of him, and to pray so earnestly for him as, by His grace, I was enabled to do. I love Him for letting me touch with my rough hand a sweet plant that He was going to transplant into paradise."

V.

Letters.

LETTERS.

CORRESPONDENCE with Christian friends now grew large, from which some extracts are subjoined below, to illustrate the course of the inner life, which they display. Every letter was winged with prayer, and became a blessing. His open spirit shunned reserve, as it abhorred ostentation; and, by unfolding itself to those whom he loved, continually promoted that real union and fellowship of saints for which he prayed, and edified his brethren. For to glance into his thoughts was to be touched with a live coal from the altar within his bosom, where burned perpetual sacrifices to God. Few indeed can lay open such a heart as his. Yet is openheartedness as desirable in the children of God as it is rare. It gives rebuke to coldness, comfort to sadness—not the less effectually because unseen. It is the foundation of fellowship and love.

"*July* 2, 1857.—You will rejoice with me, that I have had great mercies this vacation; some very sharp tribulation, but that in the world, not in Jesus: for though I have sadly obscured by my sinfulness the unclouded joy and peace which would otherwise have been mine, yet He has not let the inner joy be unfelt for long, or the foundation of deep peace be uptorn at all. . . . . Dear friend, He would have us glory in tribulation. He has determined to bless us all exceeding abundantly, and He will do it in His own gracious way. I believe He will be pleased to pour out such a blessing on His faithful, waiting Church ere long, that there shall not be room enough to receive it. Let us pray mightily for the promised outpouring of the Holy Ghost. Oh, my dear friend, we shall never have time till eternity be here, to praise Him for all the mighty works that He has done for us *already*. I seem to see such wonders crowded into the three past years of His dealings with me, as quite overwhelm me with amazement."

"BANGOR, *July* 29, 1857.—God loves to see us praise and bless Him for the little wayside treats that He prepares for His dear ones all along the path they go; not that the little things are much in themselves, but much in recalling to our thoughts the constant minute and intimate watch that our dear Father keeps over us, so that the hairs of our head are all numbered.

"The Lord seems to have been taking most loving and patient pains to instruct me this long vacation. He cannot instruct us without giving some tribulation in the flesh and in the world; but, oh! how gracious of Him, this being so, yet to melt our hearts, every now and then, by the tenderest loving-kindness! 'In the world ye shall have tribulation,'—'in me ye shall have peace.' In quoting this, I know I am going over old ground; but I have felt so very much comfort and blessing from this truth, that I am content to weary you with it."

"*August* 29, 1857.—Jesus, I am assured, never so yearns and has His bowels so moved over us as when we are tortured by the cruel motions of sin. 'They that are Christ's have crucified the flesh, with the affections and lusts.' This is a text that the Spirit has been whispering in my ears, I could almost truly say, hundreds of times; and it has never failed to do battle with this rebellious flesh.

"May the Lord Jesus draw near to your soul with indescribable comfort, speaking to you through the

Spirit out of the still depths of His love! It is sweet to pray these blessed prayers for each other."

"BANGOR, *Sept.* 17, 1857.—I took your letter with me, as I often do, to read during a solitary ramble, and so to have full opportunity of holding converse with Jesus Himself over it. Then at last I got to a lonely bit of rock and moor overlooking the mountains, and sat down, and read and much enjoyed the thirteenth and fourteenth of Numbers, to which you directed me. Jesus gave me some grapes of Eshcol that afternoon. I have begun to realize that our enemies are 'bread for us,' (Numb. xiv. 9.)

"There is a deeply solemn truth conveyed in the words, 'Lay up for yourselves treasures in heaven.' The wise Christian will be the most greedy, grasping, avaricious man, to speak as a fool, possible; he will be ever striving to be 'rich toward God.'"

To another friend he writes about the same time:—

"Dear K——, what a solemn and awful thing it is to be a Christian! we must go on, on, on; to look back is fatal, and I trust to us, through having the everlasting arms about us, impossible. Dear brother, we all want to be more *holy*, to know the meaning of those words, 'But I will forewarn you whom ye shall fear: fear Him, which after He hath killed the body hath power to cast into hell; yea, I say unto you, *Fear Him.*'"

The next term at college passed by with little to mark it. It might be at this time that the anthem was sung one evening in Trinity Chapel, "Remember not the sins and offences of my youth." These words moved our dear friend to the soul, and he recalled them again and again with sighing and tears. Never did his faith in Christ make him forget the sins, whose guilt had been washed away. Rather the deep love of Christ humbled him in the dust with the sense of his own unworthiness, so that when his faith was strongest he was lowliest.

The Christmas vacation brought trial with it, and he writes of the difficulties attending intercourse with worldly minds:—

"It is hard, very hard, to glorify Him by a kind, gentle, and loving deportment, and due entering into their topics of conversation, &c., without allowing communion with Him to be interrupted and Himself to be denied. I long to be more holy; we have a fearfully carnal nature; I would have more of that holy, happy, heavenly spirit which should commend itself to those around as being of God. And yet such is the wickedness of the world, that even that would wear 'no form nor comeliness' in its eyes. It is sweet to look forward to the end."

His aims, in social intercourse, are expressed in the following words; they give excellent advice on one of the most difficult questions of Christian practice:—"I am afraid, my dear fellow, that you have often thought me troublesome for endeavouring to obtrude serious subjects of conversation at all times: would that it came more naturally to me to do so, and that my heart were always so full of sweet heavenly thoughts as to charm and beguile all around into the service of the Master that suggested them: that were indeed to be so full of 'righteousness and peace and joy in the Holy Ghost,' as in serving Christ to be both 'acceptable to God and approved of men.' But our puny attempts to serve Christ are often so choked with sin and coldness in ourselves, as rather to incur censure of sourness and gloominess than to awaken that approbation which a more heavenly-minded service would not fail to do. But even though this be so, it is better, my dear brother, is it not, to make even a poor attempt to stem the strong current of unbelief and worldliness around, than none at all? Oh, let us earnestly pray that we may not be quite carried away by this surge of ungodliness, that is swelling so very high around Christ's Church at this time. It may be that we shall have but a short time wherein we shall be able to confess Him—oh! let us choose the good part of suffering affliction with Him now, that He may then own us as His own servants, and we may rejoice before Him with 'exceeding great joy.' Dear K——, do not look with kind eye on that wicked world which would ensnare you: those are solemn words, 'The friendship of the world is enmity with God.'"

Tyrrell could not converse long on secular topics with Christian friends; he used to grow uneasy and silent, and then to turn the conversation to spiritual things. Perhaps he went too far in this, and caused a certain tension of the mind, by not allowing his thoughts to range and relieve themselves more freely. Yet it was natural as well as conscientious in him, and made his society infinitely more valuable than that of other less strenuous Christians. He was a man of one aim; his words were not occupied with the shell of religion, but with the kernel, and did more for Christ in six years than the words of some others effect in a lifetime.

The reader will pardon, it is hoped, the insertion of an anecdote narrated at length in a letter of this vacation; it so well illustrates his watchful and straightforward activity for Christ, and deep interest in the Jews.

Having gone to the railway station to welcome home some members of his family, he found that through mistake he had an hour to spare. "I took a walk into the country to spend the time, meditating as to whether the Lord had any particular reason for this arrangement, which led me to pray that He would enable me to be the means of saving a soul that night. It was a very mild evening; and as I was rather tired, I was thankful to find a place made in some railings by the roadside on purpose to allow people to sit down, some half mile out into the country. When I got to this place, I found an old woman sitting there already, and I entered into conversation with her. I soon found that she was a Christian person, as I believe. Well, I was thankful to have had my chat with her, and on getting up to go on farther into the country I said to myself, This is not the 'soul.' This encouraged me to make it a still more definite and acknowledged prayer. After some time, I returned the same way, and found another person on the same place sitting down, which was singular enough considering the time of the year and of the evening. It was a young man. I sat down, and after a moment said, 'Sir, are you prepared to meet your God?' This led us to speak of the Lord's return. I could not quite make out what kind of state he was in. He did not respond as one who knew the Lord, and yet appeared well acquainted with these matters. I was saying something of the desirableness of making sure that our sins were washed away in Christ's blood,—he had told me before, by the way, that he read his Bible every night; but he responded to this last remark by saying something about there being 'differences of opinion,' and then, as I did not seem to catch his meaning fully, he added, 'Sir, I am a Jew.' I told him how very deep and intense an interest what he said awakened in me, for that during the last six months and more it had been a very especial and earnest subject of my prayers that God would bless his nation. He told me that for some time past he had been diligently studying the Old Testament and comparing it with the New. He found that a very small part of the prophecies were fulfilled in our Lord. 'Yes,' said I, 'in His first coming, but they will all be in His second.' He said he had been reading with a view to satisfy himself as to whether Jesus were the Messiah. He spoke with great candour and seeming earnestness. He could not sympathise with the spiritualizing sense which so many Christians put on the prophecies. He quoted, 'Ten men shall take hold of the skirt of him that is a Jew.' I explained to him my view, that his nation would be employed by God as the chief instruments in the conversion of the heathen world. He wanted to know how it could be that Jesus Christ's death was the means of the salvation of the world, and yet that his people had been driven from their country as a punishment for slaying Him. I told him that God's prerogative is to overrule evil for good, and that what was evil in the intention of the perpetrators had been turned by God into a blessing. When he asked me how it was that his nation was so despised, and I rejoined,

'Because of your national sins,' he returned with a deep emphasis, 'You are right there.'

"I cannot remember the conversation at all consecutively; I told him in the course of it the story of my own conversion from infidelity; how persuaded I was that nothing but the power of the Holy Ghost could accomplish it. Then, by the way, he wanted me to explain how the Trinity could be true. I told him, that being convinced that the Bible was God's word, and that this was revealed to us in the Bible, I was enabled to accept it though I could not understand it, and to believe it reasonable enough that there should be that in the nature of God which quite surpassed our comprehension. I told him how I believed that very soon God would visit his nation, and bring them back into their own land. I spoke of the glorious future which was in store for them, acknowledged that we only get those promises through them, that the first application of them is for *them*. He told me he had commenced the study of the Old Testament in the Hebrew. He found a difficulty in the way in which so many prophecies quoted of our Lord are incorrectly quoted, and appear rather accommodations than fulfilments.

I told him their being quoted from the Septuagint accounted for this in some instances, in others I acknowledged that it *did* appear a difficulty, but that being persuaded the whole was of God, I was ready to *accept* the application of prophecy in cases where it would not have *seemed* applicable,—and you will remember there are many instances. I mentioned also how some prophecies have a more immediate and a more remote fulfilment.

"We walked together back to the station. When we parted, I told him how much I loved and prayed for his nation. He had previously expressed himself assured of my 'sincerity;' and he then thanked me very cordially for the benefit of my society, and there was a very earnest expression in his dark and yet soft eye-lashed eye as he shook hands. I thought how he was a kinsman of Jesus. Dear K——, I cannot tell you *all* my emotions arising from this incident; you will guess some of them. It was altogether managed in such a way as no one else could have managed it but the Lord; it made me wonder at Him."

Another letter says—"We have much encouragement to pray for the peace of Jerusalem, not in the way of a religious *hobby* or pet subject, which is very bad, but simply as the same as, 'Hallowed be Thy name; Thy kingdom come; Thy will be done in earth as it is in heaven.' Oh! what a great part this of the prayer taught us by Him who spake as never man spake!"

These last words are very suggestive. Do we all realize that Jesus meant the future and complete, as well as the present and partial, fulfilment of each of those three clauses, to be prayed for by His disciples? Have we all honestly inquired at the oracles of God what part the despised Jews are intended to play in the complete fulfilment? It is worth while for us to examine what it was worth while for God to reveal.

Early in 1858, Tyrrell passed the Senate House examination, and took the degree of B.A. He intended to remain at Cambridge after this, and to read divinity there, but he had already over-read himself, and finding his health failing, he left Cambridge for home, where he fell ill. This illness, and the heavenly support which he enjoyed under it, has been already noticed. The peculiar trials of it arose from its seat—the brain and nervous system, the disorders of which unsettle the whole mind and feelings, and sometimes render the ordinary course of pious thought, feeling, and action, impossible. These trials beset him more and more thickly during the remainder of his life, and often cast him into deep waters. But Tyrrell never yielded up his faith again to this temptation, as he had done two years before. Whatever conflicts harassed him, he knew that his only hope was in Christ, and that Christ had done all for him—that he was safe in the arms of the Redeemer, who had sought and saved him when a lost sheep. He tells us that he prayed more earnestly now than at any former period of his life; and in the day that he cried God heard him, and strengthened him with strength in his soul.

It may be right to add another extract regarding this time of trial, which illustrates the inseparable connexion between a very deep sense of guilt and a full appreciation of the value of Christ's death :—

"During this spring, the Lord has been shewing me the same extreme and unfathomable wickedness in my own heart as He did two years ago; but He has of His great mercy lifted up the standard of His Spirit against it. It has not been *so* distressing a time, praise be to the goodness and faithfulness of the Lord; but it has been a sore and most distressing conflict. On one side, has been my own most corrupt heart, with its two old strongholds—lust and pride, and the love of this present world with them, and there has been Satan near, prompting, suggesting, tormenting, reproaching, vexing, oppressing, *all but* triumphing. On the other, there has been Jesus Christ, the same yesterday, to-day, and for ever. His peace He has never taken away from me, according to His word, 'In me ye shall have peace.' His presence has continually 'gone with me, and given me rest;' the angel of His presence has saved me.

"My dear brother, I cannot describe to you the depths of guilt that I have discovered in my soul; I have had fairly to bid the land goodbye, and strike out, far out of my depth, in a sea of blood. Oh! I have found a preciousness in the blood of Jesus which I never knew before; I have had, as it were, to bathe, and bathe, and bathe in His blood.

"God has been thus gently and faithfully, yet solemnly, laying His hand upon my sins. Oh! how infinitely good it is of our Father thus to endeavour to heal us of our iniquities. He gives the blood of

Jesus to wash our guilt away, but He must also teach us the exceeding sinfulness of sin; and this our hearts are generally too hard and stubborn to learn, even from what Jesus suffered for us; till we have to taste some of its bitter fruit. This gentle dealing on our Father's part displays a strange and wonderful love, forgiving us all that great debt, and only seriously and quietly laying His hand upon us, saying, as it were, 'It is all forgiven, *but that is what sin is.*'"

"Ye that love the Lord, *hate evil.*"

IV.

Last Two Years.

LAST TWO YEARS.

In April 1858, Tyrrell returned again to college, and matured his future plans, under God's guidance. His fervent desire was to preach Christ to the heathen, and he recognized that call of God to missionary labours, to which so few are disposed to listen. Accordingly, when he finally left Cambridge and all its hallowed associations behind him in June, he offered his services to the Church Missionary Society. Mr Venn saw his value, but the physician pronounced the vessel too fragile for present use. Tyrrell was therefore desired by the committee to remain in England awhile, till God should see fit to confirm his broken health. But this was never to be; almighty love and wisdom had designed some more excellent thing. The last-mentioned illness put the finishing stroke to the shattering of his constitution, beneath which he gradually decayed. He sought restoration in change of air, and went over to Ireland; thence returning to his former quarters and friends at Bangor. The outward man, however, perished; but the inward man was renewed day by day. His activity for Christ, in the midst of his weakness, was surprising. No opportunities were lost; coach, steamer, hotel, railway carriage, or quiet footpath, were not out of place or season to him for prayers and ministrations. Everywhere Jesus was on his lips; and his prayers arose for all with whom he had any intercourse.

His intercessions were astonishing to ordinary Christians. One list made for assisting his memory in prayer, perhaps about this period, contains more names than the writer can venture to state from memory, but the number must have been at least three hundred. Another and earlier list, following a brief family prayer, contains just two hundred names, and among them memorials of his travels and conversations, such as, "Boy, Burntisland;" "Soldier, Stirling passage;" "Old man, coach, Loch Awe;" "Officer and his lady, Glencoe;" "Guide on Loch ——;" "Three maids, ——." Among a few names of public notoriety is one interesting and sad, "Alfred Tennyson."

These names were not recited as if by rosary, for no intercessions were ever more full and special, for the needs of each particular person, than our dear friend's. He sends, in a letter from Bangor, July 13, 1858, directions for special prayer in his own behalf, and adds, "In thus specifying to you some points, I treat you as I should like to be treated; and we have St Paul's frequent example of being definitive in prayers."

It is not intended here to unveil some private plans and troubles which commenced about this period. Tyrrell acted most conscientiously throughout them, but suffered not a little from uncertainty and unkindness.

"*Oct.* 13, 1858.—I trust that God will keep me nailed to this cross; in order that, being in truth crucified with Christ, the life which I now live in the flesh I may live by faith in the Son of God. Meantime, I have found that the more the sufferings of Christ have thus abounded in me, so much the more also has my consolation abounded by Christ, so that I often rejoice with joy unspeakable and full of glory: and the more I have decreased, so much the more has Christ increased." "Stir up all the brethren at Cambridge still perseveringly to wait on God for the outpouring of His Spirit."

"*Nov.* 25, 1858.—About having to learn to lean on Christ alone, you say truly, truly, truly. It is good for us to feel experimentally that 'verily *every man at his best estate* is *altogether* vanity'—that God is all and man nothing." In this letter he expresses gratitude for relief from his chief trials.

"*Jan.* 6, 1859.—God's chastisements are good. Oh! how wonderful is that mingled severity and gentleness with which He leads us on to a city that hath foundations. I seem daily to see more of His unutterable love, as manifested in the correction which He bestows on His sin-ruined and yet beloved creatures."

Soon after this last letter was written, Tyrrell paid a fortnight's visit to the writer's family. He soon won all hearts with his kind, gentle ways, sweet smiles, and humble, unaffected piety. At first somewhat depressed and silent, he soon improved in spirits, and talked freely, not without vivacity and fun like his former self. But he never liked the conversation to stray far from religion; or to leave his Saviour out of His due place in the enjoyments of a Christian family; thus we all felt the benefit of our dear friend's presence.

He did not wish to be personally idle, and inquired where his visits to the poor would be of most service. He was directed to a poor young man dying of consumption, who seemed to be a hardened self-deceiver, although he had lived a bad life; and was very difficult of access. Tyrrell went to see him four times, but was as often purposely avoided. Any one else would have given up the case at once; but after praying much for the unfortunate youth, Tyrrell penned the long letter from which the account of his conversion has been already taken, and which contains much language of loving appeal besides what has been cited. This letter was written from London after he had left us. It touched the sufferer's heart, and induced better feelings; but he sank soon afterwards, without giving *clear* evidences of conversion.

Tyrrell writes to one who had long attended the sick-room—"Concerning poor M——, I could not help rejoicing, though the joy was mixed with sorrow and regret. You expressed the truth concerning him most happily when you said, 'there was much to hope for, but nothing to glory in.'"

And again:—"My song, in this, is of mercy and judgment—mercy, because I hope and believe that there was a work of God's Spirit in his soul; of judgment, because He did not allow me to have undoubted evidence of the fact. Perhaps it was the possibility of our glorying in something that prevented our heavenly Father from being able to let us *see* more satisfactory reason to rejoice."

Tyrrell now arranged to live in Brixton with a college friend, with the view of "helping him in his work (of visiting the poor), having the advantage of the ministry of a very good man, and being within reach of country walks." Thither he went after leaving us amid many regrets on both sides, and saying, "I shall always look back on this visit as one of the happiest periods in my life." So dearly did he prize that free Christian communion which had been rarely granted him on earth.

The following sketch is from the pen of the friend above-mentioned:—"I can never be sufficiently thankful for that overruling Providence which led dear Tyrrell to be with me at Brixton for so long.

He used to be my counsellor and friend, to whom I could communicate all my spiritual trials, and talk with him about my parish. Every morning we used to read together and plead together at the throne of grace. He could not attempt much work in the parish, but his life was itself a sermon. He seemed to live on his knees, his Bible his constant companion; he did not read much besides. He was very fond of D'Aubigne's 'Reformation.' A life so hid with Christ in God, could not but compel all men to acknowledge that he had been with Jesus: the peace of God seemed to keep his heart and mind, and even those who could not *understand* him, appeared to feel the power of his life; they were all so pleased with his quiet, kind, gentle bearing. In our walks together into the country, he delighted to speak on the works of his Father; his eyes were open to the beauties of creation." It might be added, that he loved also to rise from the seen to the unseen. The sun, moon, and stars were associated in many a parable to him; the soft blue sky brought to his lips the question, "What does that remind you of? The love of Christ!" And sunset glories, with their pictured plains and hills, revived his anticipations of heaven:—

"O God! O good beyond compare!
If thus Thy meaner works are fair—
If thus Thy bounties gild the span
Of ruined earth and sinful man,
How glorious must the mansions be
Where Thy redeemed shall dwell with Thee!"

He greatly rejoiced at the news of the awakening in Ireland, when assured of its genuine character. Hearing from Coleraine that all religious books were eagerly caught up, and that more were greatly wanted, he first sent a large packet of tracts, and afterwards, nearly all his religious books. He took great interest in Mr Muller's Orphan Asylum at Ashley Down, Clifton; he sent more than one box of articles to be sold for their benefit, including all his silver and little valuable things which he had by him, and which he gave up for the Lord's sake.

Respecting the Irish revival, he writes warmly to another friend, describing it as the "*present and powerful operation of the Holy Spirit of God.*" "The physical manifestations which have been exhibited in these converts one might wish absent, but we cannot tie down God to do His work otherwise than as He will. 'By their fruits ye shall know them,' is a test which these occurrences will most triumphantly bear. My own soul has been filled with praise, with joy unspeakable and full of glory, at the manner in which God has been Himself doing, with His own right hand and with His holy arm, the work that none but He can do.". "We should pray that the Irish converts and others, wherever the Holy Spirit be pleased to work, may be preserved from all the snares and delusions of Satan, may be sober-minded, quiet, and preserved from fanatical enthusiasm, to which the human heart is always exposed when the emotions are very strongly moved. I believe that we shall see ere long how fully and abundantly the God that heareth prayer designs to answer the many supplications, that have been ascending before Him for a true and deep revival of religion. You remember, dear brother, how we used the expressions (in prayer,) 'exceeding abundantly,' 'according to the riches of His glory,' 'open the windows of heaven;' and if *we* remember them, shall God have forgotten them?"

And with regard to the Orphan Asylum, the writer is aware that it was the piety and *believing prayers* of the founder that first drew forth Tyrrell's hearty sympathy and support.

Our hopes of the restoration of his health had risen with his own. But they were rudely dashed to the ground again, when, after an intermittence of correspondence, he wrote from his bed, on March 31, 1859, that he had had a severe attack of neuralgia and bilious fever. "I have been nearer the gates than ever, except once." . . . "He has been the same gracious, faithful God, upholding me, and preventing me from thinking hardly of Him."

Not many incidents relating to Tyrrell's residence at Brixton have reached the writer; indeed, he was so shattered in health, that he could talk and visit but little, and was tried by the discipline of patience. A few extracts from letters, however, will shew how patience had her perfect work in him.

"BRIXTON, *April* 12, 1859.—It was 'loving correction'—infinitely kind it is of Him to bestow it upon me. The work that He has been doing in my soul for some time past has, I trust, been, in some measure, the deepening of my conviction of sin. I have needed, and still need, very much on this head. I think I have had more felt communion with the adorable person of the Spirit of God than previously."

"*May* 5, 1859.—That is a sweet promise, 'I will be with him in trouble.' I trust I have, in some measure, learnt to praise and bless God for His chastisements. It has pleased Him to bring me somewhat deeply, since my conversion, into the fellowship of Christ's sufferings; and I am now only beginning to see how entirely indispensable that suffering has been, and beyond this, to count it as a settled thing that this will not be otherwise till I meet the Lord face to face.

"For a long time past the threefold subject of my prayers has been—the outpouring of the Holy Spirit, the Jews, and the union of all believers."

"BRIXTON, *July* 29, 1859.—I hope that this little dispensation of on-waiting, which I have frequently felt trying, will have the use which it was designed to have, in teaching me patiently to wait upon God, and more really to trust *Him*, and not circumstances. I have been surprised to find, when thus put a little to the test, how far I have been from really trusting God himself, rather than the means by which He is wont to work.

"I think I have been enabled to enter somewhat more than ever before into the meaning of that blessed relationship to God as our '*Father.*' Catching some little glimpse of what our 'Father' is, has given me a sad sight of the deep alienation from God in which we are by nature sunk. I have been led to feel what a miracle of grace it is, ('what is the exceeding greatness of His power,') to enable any poor lost child of Adam to get back to the position of trust in God as our Father. Truly the country into which we prodigals have been straying is a far country—very, very far off from our Father's house."

The following interesting remarks on the right use of Scripture, and particularly of the Old Testament, were elicited by a friend's questioning his application of the passage on Divine wisdom in Proverbs to prove the pre-existence of Christ:—(chap. viii.)

"Let us, first of all, establish doctrine by plain, undeniable Scripture; let us next support by scripturally authenticated types; and then let us, if we will, set forth, illustrate, pictorially impress, by Scriptures which only the spiritually-illumined understanding is so led to apply. With regard to Christ's pre-existence, I suppose we have fifty plain statements of the fact in the New Testament."

"The sense in which the Old Testament Scriptures testify of Christ is truly a multitudinous one: I suppose in nothing so much as by way of *contrast;* for instance, when we read in Judges, again and again, 'They did evil,' 'They did evil,' with what gratitude does the heart fly to that better covenant ratified in Christ, '*I will put my laws in their hearts!*' Oh, how deeply and continually thankful should we be, that God has made us partakers of a dispensation, in which He no longer waits to see 'what man can do, and finds that man can do nothing,' but comes forward Himself to meet the utter helplessness and ruin of man by undertaking the whole matter from first to last Himself! What a blessed plan of salvation!"

In the summer, Tyrrell was ordered to seek manual labour, for exercise' sake, in another residence. He continued his inquiries for several months, and unremitting prayers for guidance, that God might open to him a pious home. This was providentially found at last on Mitcham Common, whither he removed on August 20. Soon afterwards his letters expressed the deepest thankfulness for the truly

Christian character of his new friends with whom he lodged, and he praised God.

"It is particularly sweet, thank-inspiring, refreshing, and encouraging, to look back upon between three and four months of waiting upon God, often in faintness and readiness to give up, and then to see the full, sure, yea, bountiful answer at length. Oh, magnify the Lord with me, and let us exalt His name together!"

Never did the twentieth day of any month pass by at Mitcham without his giving thanks to God for this gracious answer to prayer. While there, he used to spend some hours a-day in visiting the cottages, conversing with the poor, and leaving tracts. But his health did not improve much, nor always permit even this exertion.

"MITCHAM, *Dec.* 19, 1859.—I believe that the binding together of those who are really Christ's, in common separation from and uncompromising opposition to the world, is an object unspeakably dear to our exalted Lord above; I believe there is no consummation so devoutly to be prayed for by His members below, and none that will more speedily and effectually make for the hastening of His king dom."

The writer spent a week with him at Ramsgate soon after this date, and saw how worn and wasted was the outward man, and the soul still tried through the weakness of the flesh. Yet his spirituality and tenderness were greater than ever, his peace unshaken, Christ near and loved, and himself increasingly conformed to the image of Jesus.

"*Jan.* 21, 1860.—I must take advantage of this unrelentingly rainy morning to write one more brief letter, to assure you that my love is longer than my pen. Thank you, dear brother, for your kind wishes in reference to the new year. I am looking for a very happy year this year. I fondly hope and believe that it will be a happy year to the whole Church of God, and a year when the songs of the angels will be swelled with joy over a great multitude of lost ones brought home."

The following beautiful words are a touching conclusion to a long and precious intercourse; they occur at the end of the last letter to the writer, dated Feb. 23, 1860:—

"My love for your relations and others, to whom I write but sparingly, is of no evanescent kind, flowing down as it does from the heart of Him who abideth ever, and destined, as I trust it is, to last till it issue into that flood of bridal joy, which awaits the members of Christ's body at the marriage-supper of the Lamb."

Since the above was written, a letter dated Mitcham, April 11, 1860, has been received, from the friend to whom it was addressed. It shews such cheerfulness of spirit, that we would fain hope God had mercifully given a rest and calm of spirit to our deeply-tried brother in Christ, so that at his evening time there was light.

"I often thought of dear K—— yesterday; in the evening, as I walked home from a little prayer-meeting in the village, the bells were ringing in honour of the occasion," (the wedding of his friend); "my thoughts were carried to him in his happiness, and then they were carried on to that happier time when the bells of all creation will ring for the marriage-supper of the Lamb. Who shall tell the joys and glories of that wondrous time, when the Lord of glory shall be wedded for ever to the whole vast assembly of His blood-bought people! Does it not seem that the 'midnight cry' is even now being heard? Does not the awakening of slumbering Christendom seem sometimes very like that of the virgins, wise and foolish, who arose and trimmed their lamps?"

Our dear friend felt more poorly than usual in April, and after a few days' deliberation and prayer, —his invariable practice,—left Mitcham for Ventnor in the Isle of Wight, on the 25th of April. On the 27th he wrote thence:—

"I am not feeling strong enough to do more than write one line to you to tell you of the Lord's loving care over me hitherto. . . . The Lord brought me most graciously through the journey, and gave me sufficient strength to enjoy it. The day was spent mostly alone with the Lord. I did not feel fitted for much conversation. But I had a long talk with a Christian woman on the coach between Ryde and Ventnor. She seemed nicely taught, realized her acceptance with God through the Lord Jesus, and looked for His return. She lives close to the little church at St Lawrence, is the wife of a coastguardsman, would be glad to see me if I should walk that way; so I took her address, and hope to see her again. The scenery along the coast was unexpectedly lovely. The Lord most kindly provided for me, so that I was heard in that I feared, both with respect to the weather and lodging. He has been very kind to me, as He is wont."

He mentions a painful swelling of the throat, but by no means anticipates serious consequences from it. However, as he was not better on Saturday, the medical man was called in, who pronounced the disease to be typhus fever. He became worse about midnight on Saturday night, but did not appear to be in any great pain; his greatest suffering seemed to be the feeling of extreme weakness. He was most patient; not a murmur escaped his lips. This also was an answer to his expressed desire and prayer, that in the sufferings of death he might never dishonour Christ by impatience.

About half-past four the morning of the Sabbath began to dawn; he seemed to see it directly, and said with difficulty, "Behold the morning cometh." He desired to be prayed for at the Sunday-morning service, and quoted 2 Cor. ix. 8, "And God is able to make all grace abound toward you; that ye, always having all sufficiency in all things, may abound to every good work," to the kind friend who attended him. Still he did not appear to think his sickness would be unto death. He manifested to those who attended his sick-bed extreme resignation and thankfulness for their attention, expressing no wish as to the issue of his illness. His only desire was that his friend Mr A——, at Mitcham, might be sent for.

On the morning of Monday, April 30, when the nurse raised him in bed, he lifted his eyes and said, "What will it be to dwell above, and with the Lord of glory reign?" After this he lay down, apparently more comfortable than he had been for many hours. Gradually he became insensible, and at two o'clock P.M. fell asleep in Jesus, so gently that his spirit had long fled ere the friend who held his hand became aware of it. So tenderly did the Father of mercies spare the pains of death to his long-tried servant.

His remains rest in Brading Cemetery, beneath the text, "To live is Christ, and to die is gain."

"Blessed are the dead which die in the Lord from henceforth: yea, saith the Spirit, for they rest from their labours, and their works do follow them."

The subjoined hymn was copied by our dear friend, probably as a special favourite, and not long before his death, which literally and unexpectedly realized the anticipations expressed in it:—

"Thou wilt shew me the path of life."—Ps. xvi. 11.

"I love yon pale blue sky; it is the floor
Of that glad home where I shall shortly be;
A home from which I shall go out no more;
From toil and grief and vanity set free.

"I gaze upon yon everlasting arch,
Up which the bright stars wander, as they shine;
And as I mark them in their nightly march,
I think how soon that journey shall be mine.

"Yon silver drift of silent cloud, far up
In the still heaven,—through you my pathway lies!
Yon rugged mountain-peak,—how soon your top
Shall I behold beneath me, as I rise!

"Not many more of life's slow-pacing hours,
Shaded with sorrow's melancholy hue;
Oh, what a glad ascending shall be ours,
Oh, what a pathway up yon starry blue!

"A journey like Elijah's, swift and bright,
Caught gently upward to an early crown,
In heaven's own chariot of all-blazing light,
With death untasted and the grave unknown."

BONAR.

BALLANTYNE AND COMPANY, PRINTERS, EDINBURGH.

Milton Keynes UK
Ingram Content Group UK Ltd.
UKHW020954211124
3018UKWH00044B/603